INTERIOR VISIONS

INTERIOR VISIONS

Mona Hajj

FOREWORD BY ALLAN GREENBERG

TEXT WRITTEN WITH MARC KRISTAL

THE MONACELLI PRESS

CONTENTS

FOREWORD

I had never worked with Mona Hajj when I recommended her to one of my clients, the Embassy of Luxembourg in Washington, D.C. We had met once or twice, and my intuition told me that she was the right person for the project, the renovation and redesign of the interiors. Embassy interiors are far more difficult to design than houses. Each nation, working through its ambassadors and administrative staff, has a distinctive sense of how it wishes to present itself. Calibrating this quality challenging. When it is there, we all feel it; when it is not, it is difficult to say why. Mona's sense of what was right was nearly flawless. She perceived nuances of character and meaning that often eluded me, and our collaboration paved the way to a successful design.

Our partnership was marked by a mutual understanding and trust that allowed for interactive and constructive criticism. Good will and humor were present whenever we sat down to discuss problems and review progress. Looking back, I suspect we both were on the prowl for good ideas—and pleased to appropriate them irrespective of where they originated. It transformed working together into a process of learning and, therefore, a rare pleasure.

Why has a vigorous and nourishing give-and-take between architects and interior designers come to be such a rarity? It remains a mystery why our respective professions don't foster improved mutual understanding in schools and professional associations. Instead, we stand fast and battle for control, fostering an atmosphere of suspicion and vulnerability. Perhaps it is the large overlap between our spheres of interest that provides so many opportunities for quarrels over territory. We share concerns with the character of the house; with the placement, size, and character of windows and doors; with room shapes and their connections to adjacent spaces; with movement patterns and relationships between interiors and exterior, house and garden. In short, the integrity of our designs is, to a large extent, dependent on each other's work.

Collaboration requires courage. A true partnership entails sharing control, but our two professions remain fearful of such a prospect. Surely the great collaborations of Stanford White and Elsie de Wolfe, Le Corbusier and Charlotte Perriand, David Adler and Frances Adler Elkins, and Mies van der Rohe and Lilly Reich were built on an intense commitment to learn from each other. Working with Mona was a paradigm of the mutually fruitful and respectful working relationship that should be more common between our fields.

As is amply illustrated by the luscious photographs in this book, Mona is a master of interior design. Her choices of colors, fabrics, and furnishings and her marvelous sense of scale transform even the most mundane of rooms into a magical kingdom. She is a rare and gifted woman, and it has been my privilege to work with her. Now it is an even greater privilege for me to introduce to you, dear reader, the work of this wonderful and amazing artist.

—*Allan Greenberg*

PREFACE

I have always loved the idea that antique Persian rugs—which are among my most favorite things in the world—were woven by people who, while following a plan and working within a system, also made room in the process for discovery and improvisation. While they began with an idea, they allowed their imagination to take them to unexpected places, destinations that became part of the grand design. To a remarkable extent, the great Persian rug weavers discovered what they were making by making it.

Perhaps I appreciate this because my own method is, in some respects, quite similar. I work closely with my clients to create homes that will delight them, but I never begin with a determined plan. For me, interior design is all about how things feel instinctively, the special magic that flourishes when different elements are joined together. This leap of faith can be difficult for new clients to accept. Yet the people I have worked with repeatedly understand and embrace this way of creating. Like the Persian rug weavers, I discover what I am making by making it—and inevitably, the result is personal to my client, pleasurable to inhabit, and unique.

OPPOSITE: *In this Rehoboth, Delaware, dining room, I matched a casual nineteenth-century trestle table with more formal antique chairs. A suzani textile hanging serves as art.*

This last is particularly important to me. Though there are certain common threads that run through my work—rugs being foremost among them—I don't have a "look" and have never tried to develop one. A home is the most personal of possessions, and to brand it with name fabrics or furnishings—or to do it in a recognizable style—is to make the dwelling less rather than more my clients' own. If I have a philosophy, it is to work with my clients to seek out the unknown or undefined—things that aren't meant to impress or make a statement but rather enable them to live amid beauty, comfort, and serenity.

So please, don't look here for a signature style—or even for too much seriousness. I consider what I do—meeting interesting people, discovering how they like to live, and searching the world and its cultures for beautiful and unusual elements—to be a privilege, a pleasure, and a great deal of fun. I hope you will look at my work in a similar spirit: as an ongoing creative journey that is its own reason for being.

OPPOSITE: *An antique English gilded console anchors this Baltimore foyer. A Tiffany lamp sits comfortably by an Indian horse sculpture.*

FORMAL TABLEAUS

Architecture is always my first inspiration, and so my formal projects derive from formal architecture. But while I love the classical, I find that it can sometimes be too rigid. The truth is that I hate perfection—I always want a room to feel human. So into formal settings I try to introduce a twist.

For example, in a house by John Russell Pope, who designed the National Archives and Jefferson Memorial in Washington, D.C., I eliminated the overwhelmingly diverse color palette, which is considered more correct, and painted everything a creamy white—walls, ceilings, pilasters—updating the architecture by making it a beautiful silhouette. Then I introduced such unexpected elements as a Syrian chest of drawers and a Rococo mirror—objects that don't relate directly to the architecture but still respect it, and live comfortably and beautifully within it.

Indeed, there's no reason why even the most serious spaces, such as a ceremonial receiving room, can't also be welcoming. Many people never go into their living rooms—but why have one and not enjoy it? Why use the dining room only when you have guests? I believe you are your own best company and that even a formal dining room can be comfortable, inviting, and approachable.

Most important, for me, are the people for whom I'm creating a design. Formality at thirty means something different from formality at sixty, and I always try to respect the difference.

OPPOSITE: Charlcote, the Baltimore residence of James Swan Frick, was designed by the neoclassicist John Russell Pope and completed in 1915. For a young couple, I adjusted the formal interiors to reflect their more relaxed way of life.

There is a difference
between formality and
solemnity. Since most people
prefer their homes to be
approachable rather than
intimidating, I try to achieve,
in formal settings, a quality
of relaxed elegance.

RIGHT: *I love color, but for Charlcote's main*
foyer, I chose a simple cream since there was
sufficient beauty and intricacy to be found in the
architecture. A sixteen-foot-wide eighteenth-century
bookcase adds drama to the soothing tableau.

ABOVE: *A study for the wife mixes Charlcote's authoritative original millwork with softer colors and comfortable seating.* OPPOSITE: *In the main foyer, also a reception area, I placed a contemporary sofa near the front door so that visitors might wait in comfort.*

ABOVE AND OPPOSITE: *The foyer of this 1916 Renaissance Revival residence in Maryland was compact, but big enough for an eighteenth-century Italian canapé adorned with pillows covered in embroidered antique lampas fabric. The settee's reflective silk taffeta lightens the mood, as does the eighteenth-century Venetian chandelier.*

ABOVE: *The architecture of this Georgian Revival farmhouse on Maryland's eastern shore, built in the 1920s, is simple and sublime. A table and chairs at the top of the stairs create a moment of repose at the junction of two circulation spaces.*
OPPOSITE: *A painted Regency cane settee provides the ideal complement in the foyer.*
OVERLEAF: *Comfortable seating and curvilinear furnishings and objects make the living room of a Chevy Chase, Maryland, house inviting and user-friendly.*

ABOVE: *An unusual—and lively—tole lantern brightens the entry of the Chevy Chase residence.*
OPPOSITE: *A nineteenth-century secretary commands a corner of the living room.* OVERLEAF: *Opposite the secretary is a hand-painted antique leather screen. A curved sofa both establishes and anchors the seating area.*

Comfortable furniture
upholstered in simple
fabrics, cheerful colors,
arrangements that foster
conviviality—with a few
simple gestures, even the
most buttoned-up
environment can be easy
and pleasurable to inhabit.

RIGHT: *In the Embassy of Luxembourg in*
Washington, D.C., the library features bookmatched
panels and a patterned ceiling. Decorative additions
include a simple chandelier, custom-designed
wrought-iron-and-wood cocktail tables, and an
ottoman upholstered in an antique Turkish textile.

ABOVE: *In the embassy's entry, an antique Persian gallery rug and a wrought-iron-and-gold-leaf lantern enhance the preexisting furnishings.* OPPOSITE: *An unexpected touch—raffia window shades—appears in a bay in the study.*
OVERLEAF: *To the embassy reception room, I added a nineteenth-century crystal chandelier and an antique Persian rug. The soft, neutral paint colors provide a soothing background, as do the simple silk velvet drapery panels.*

RIGHT: *The ornate crystal chandelier in this Chevy Chase dining room offsets the simplicity of the Regency table. Warm background colors, an antique rug, and a contemplative seascape add to the intimate mood.*

RIGHT: *I ordinarily avoid faux finishes, but the family room in the Chevy Chase house invited such a treatment. We warmed up the background with tone-on-tone color and a decorative vine motif. A damask Roman shade completes the picture.*

ABOVE AND OPPOSITE: *In the living room of this Georgian-style farmhouse, built in 1930, silk-and-linen drapery panels, sturdy child-friendly upholstery, and an informal Aubusson rug establish the ideal mood for a summer home.*

Classical architecture, thoughtfully conceived and executed, is a great gift. In a private room, it is the small details that infuse it with intimacy.

RIGHT: *This master suite sitting room, in a farmhouse on Maryland's eastern shore, avoids fancy furnishings in favor of a relaxed, welcoming decor. The pale celadon color and curved velvet-covered sofa set the mood. Late-nineteenth-century sconces flank the painting above the fireplace.*

ABOVE AND OPPOSITE: *To compress the length of this living room, in a house in Chevy Chase, I anchored the four corners of the space with custom bookcases and created several sitting areas. Comfortable overstuffed seating makes this a model environment for large gatherings, and the nineteenth-century American convex mirror helps guests keep an eye on one another.*

ABOVE AND OPPOSITE: *This farmhouse dining room is both formal and—thanks to a nineteenth-century Baccarat chandelier— somewhat opulent. But because my clients often dine alone, I developed a casual dining area, complete with cozy wing chairs, beside the fireplace. The painting and demilune table crowd the drapes a bit, but if you love something you can always find a way to make it work.*

ABOVE AND OPPOSITE: *For this outdoor living area, we combined formal and informal furnishings and arrangements to complement the Italianate flavor of the architecture.*

Sometimes a furniture piece is a bit—or more than a bit— too big or too small. But so what? Things don't have to be perfect to be enjoyed. For me, if a room and its contents feel good, then they *are* good.

RIGHT: *In this guest bedroom in Baltimore, I devised a romantic setting with a nineteenth-century hand-painted Venetian Rococo bed, French lace linens, and upholstered furnishings.*

ABOVE: *I restyled the chaise in a master bedroom in Baltimore into something of a design oddity—an armchair with a long nose.* OPPOSITE: *A nineteenth-century Italian coverlet and a silk damask tablecloth over the night table create romance in a farmhouse bedroom.*

SERENE SETTINGS

I have said that I have many favorite things. But serenity is my favorite of favorites. The lives we lead today are dynamic, busy, full of travel and activity. When you go home, you want to enter a private realm that really calms you down—a place that's inviting, that you never want to leave. Serenity, in a word, is peace. And I try to interject it into all my interiors.

For many people, a serene home means something Zen or Asian—very spare and simple. Yet while I love and respect Eastern design, life is different in the West—we like things, and have more of them. While simplicity may be a source of serenity, so too are luxury and sumptuousness. Serenity in design can also be captured with more levels and textures, more complex interiors.

What are these? Beautiful fabrics and rugs. Spaces that embrace natural light. Well-crafted objects and furnishings that offer a sense of solidity and care. Personal moments—a chair by a window where you can sit and let your mind wander. Variations of texture convey serenity, too, as do comfortably scaled pieces and walls finished in soothing colors. And falling into lush, embracing cushions. Even artworks impart serenity, such as the landscape I hung over a client's bed—it included two sheep for counting.

Whatever feels good—that is guaranteed to produce serenity. But only if it's well lit. I always say that God created the world—and then he made dimmer switches.

OPPOSITE: *In one corner of a Baltimore living room, I combined an eighteenth-century Austrian secretary, a Tabríz carpet, and soft colors with a magical ingredient—sunlight—to foster a moment of blissful repose.*

A harmoniously composed room serves as a quiet background for the life within it, receding so that people can relax and enjoy themselves. A surface that captures and reflects light infuses the environment with soothing warmth.

RIGHT: *Simple upholstered seating mixes with a diversity of international furnishings—a nineteenth-century Italian trestle table, a Japanese gold-leaf-paneled screen, and a Biedermeier clock from Austria—to produce a living room ideal for both social gatherings and quiet contemplation.* OVERLEAF: *The lively unruliness of a canvas by Betty Holliday complements the strongly axial design of this New York living room. The look is architectural and modern, but the flavor is comfortable and timeless.*

OPPOSITE AND ABOVE: *In the New York apartment, objects and artifacts—notably the ebony elephant head in the window, discovered in Africa by my world-traveling client—arrest and delight the eye.*

ABOVE: *A sculptor friend of my client created the grouping of metal "branches."*
OPPOSITE: *The textile behind the African objects—with a nineteenth-century Kaitag tapestry from Dagestan at its center—conceals a very un-serene television.*

ABOVE AND OPPOSITE: *The rich blue of a French opaline chandelier, echoed in the upholstered settee, projects a strong burst of color onto the white background of this Palm Beach living room. Nineteenth-century Japanese "hawk" hand-painted gold-leaf panels flank the window.*

ABOVE: *In this Long Island residence, an antique suzani wall hanging, a Persian Sarab runner, and a very narrow bench with a window view make a transitional zone into a habitable space. In the room beyond, an abstract canvas hangs above a bench I designed.* OPPOSITE: *In the main foyer are a nineteenth-century center table and a contemporary Persian painting.*

ABOVE: *In this McLean, Virginia, living room, the strong lines of the custom-designed wrought-iron coffee table prove an effective contrast to the flowing, deep pink silk of the armchairs.* OPPOSITE: *A chair and a clock stand in the room's "Swedish" corner.*

Complementary hues,
whether rendered in fabrics,
furnishings, or wall
treatments, create a soothing
unity throughout a room.

RIGHT: *This master bedroom in Baltimore provides
peace and serenity with a monochromatic color scheme and
antique textiles. The room includes an eighteenth-century
Italian sofa with a nineteenth-century brocade and a strong
four-poster featuring a silk velvet headboard and antique
Italian hand-embroidered lace bolster. The X-base ottoman I
designed is upholstered with a French Aubusson.*

ABOVE AND OPPOSITE: *I established a visual connection between the master bedroom and bath with a pair of chaise longues that are similar in profile. The formal echo helps to make the two spaces feel like a single, continuous experience.*

LEFT: In this master suite sitting room, in a waterside house on Long Island, the uniform color palette provides an appropriately tranquil background.

ABOVE AND OPPOSITE: *The clean sculptural quality of the furnishings in the Long Island bedroom, amplified by the pattern-free fabrics, contributes to the space's soothing simplicity.*

REFINED PALETTES

For me, color is mood. Dark, rich colors create a sense of intimacy (and are very appetizing in a dining room—they make you want to eat). Blue is majestic. Bedrooms receive softer, more romantic shades. I love color, and I use it very thoughtfully—before I make a choice, I want to be sure it's one my client will want to live with.

One sure way to succeed is to follow and accentuate the natural light in a space, not to resist it. We have all heard the cliché "It's a dark room, so paint it a light color." Rather, if it's a dark room, paint it darker—you don't want to fight nature.

Similarly, I am not attracted to bold colors that announce themselves too aggressively. You can achieve the special character and mood that derives from color more effectively with a gentle approach. I try to avoid dramatic (and trendy) contrasts, preferring to layer colors that feel good together—joining wall treatments, furnishings, artworks, and textiles to achieve a result that is no less beautiful for being subtle.

In much of my work I enjoy carefully accumulating a number of small moments into a large effect—and that is especially true of my approach to color.

OPPOSITE: *The appetite-inducing red permeating the dining room in John Russell Pope–designed Charlcote is everywhere: from the walls to the chairs to the carpet—and even to the flowers.*

RIGHT: *Charlcote's dining room is materially as well as visually sumptuous, especially in the patterned antique rug—a circa 1890 Bijar—and the oversize nineteenth-century Indian sari I fashioned into a tablecloth.*

When interior architecture is strongly articulated and rich in color, bold tones are essential—not to fight the surroundings, but to complement them. A neutral palette would simply disappear.

RIGHT: *The wood paneling in the library at Charlcote had lightened with time. We restored it to its original darker shade, then further enriched the room with the blue velvet damask of the upholstery. The carpet is a Bakshaish from the 1880s.*

ABOVE: *The shades in this Baltimore library are largely red—but the dramatic Tiffany chandelier delivers a dash of blazing yellow.*
OPPOSITE: *Blue-flocked paper covers the walls and ceiling in this Chevy Chase library. The color repeats in the upholstery of the club and reading chairs. The oversize bookcase makes a good companion to the chest, with mother-of-pearl inlay, from Syria.*

ABOVE: *When the hues are all deep, as in this McLean, Virginia, family room, the "color" is neutral—in this instance,
the antique-Aubusson-covered ottoman.* OPPOSITE: *For the library of a scholar from Beirut, which brims with the books and
artifacts of a busy life, I used color to encase the visual vitality, almost as if the room were a red curio box.*

Some of the most
pleasing colors are those
found in natural
materials, such as
beautifully burnished
knotty pine, worn leather,
and antique wool.

RIGHT: *For this traditional man's lounge, in a*
farmhouse on Maryland's eastern shore, I selected
a pair of Art Deco leather armchairs, a paisley-
patterned wood Roman shade, and oak-paneled walls.

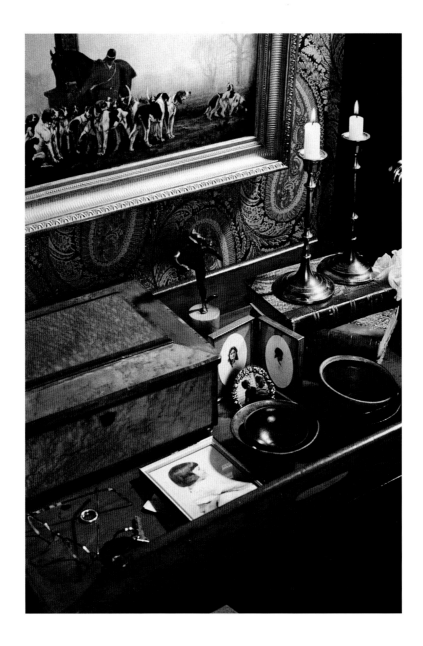

ABOVE AND OPPOSITE: *The owner of this Baltimore bedroom wanted a masculine space that was rich in color. Paisley wallpaper, two carpets, and a patterned footstool before an antique cockfighting chair answered his request.*

In a room with ample glazing and verdant views, dark walls can both make the space feel more intimate and enclosed and highlight the landscape outside the windows.

RIGHT: *This man's study is carpeted with a beautiful nineteenth-century Tabriz. An Indian dowry chest serves as a coffee table, and a Syrian game table awaits beneath a window.*

ABOVE: *One of the most adaptable colors is white, especially when it comes to making a darker shade "pop"—as is the case with the plum-colored fabric on the chairs and window seats in this Chevy Chase, Maryland, game room.* OPPOSITE: *The gently pooling drapes, made of linen and silk, and celadon walls and ceiling give the dining room/conservatory an air at once contemplative and romantic. A Regency glass-and-brass lantern is suspended above French dining chairs from the 1940s.*

Closely related neutral shades, subtly layered, give a room a surprising sense of depth and convey elegance and sophistication.

LEFT: *In this apartment in the Ritz-Carlton in Washington, D.C., I cloaked a mix of modern and antique furnishings in a soothing natural palette to create a welcoming oasis amid the hotel's hustle and bustle.*

Color is an excellent foil for modern or industrial architecture, introducing richness and warmth into what might otherwise be a hard-edged, unwelcoming environment.

ABOVE AND OPPOSITE: *Blue and gold predominate throughout the Baltimore apartment, appearing in such details as the Chinese and Delft porcelains before a 1920s French wall hanging and the embroidered nineteenth-century English fabric—actually a former table linen—on two of the canapé throw pillows.* OVERLEAF: *In the same apartment, a late-eighteenth-century inlaid Dutch kas stands in the bedroom. I had the kilim in the sitting room made in Turkey from fragments of old Persian rugs.*

While many people are reluctant to embrace color—for fear of making a mistake—it is remarkably adaptable. I try to incorporate color of many different sorts—in artworks, in fabrics—so that it all mixes harmoniously.

RIGHT: *The portrait above the fireplace—a family heirloom—establishes the mood in this living room in a waterside farmhouse on Long Island.*

ABOVE AND OPPOSITE: *Blue can mean many different things—it may be soothing, cool, or electrifying. In this New York bedroom, which is very nearly a single color, I chose shades of blue that are conducive to rest and reflection.*

ABOVE, OPPOSITE, AND OVERLEAF: *In this Long Island living room, soft blue walls provide a serene backdrop for layers of texture: hand-printed silk draperies, a Persian carpet, and a custom-designed ottoman upholstered in an antique textile. Arrangements of family photos add to the room's sense of intimacy.*

I think it's fun to do the obvious sometimes. Shades of pink and rose, let's say, support a mood that is intentionally playful and feminine.

RIGHT: *I was pleased to have a client appreciative of the old-fashioned pleasures to be derived from a room dedicated to afternoon tea. Though I typically choose more discreet flat-paneled drapes, the rose-colored chamber called for a more sumptuous treatment.*

PERSONAL VISIONS

I bought my apartment sight unseen. It sounds crazy, I know. But I love the neighborhood, a part of Baltimore called Gilford—old and comfortable, urbane yet countrified. The building, too, attracted me—a 1928 Beaux-Arts structure with the special character that comes with having good bones. But there were no availabilities. So I waited, and when I heard that a 3,500-square-foot, three-bedroom apartment was being auctioned, I grabbed it.

It was in terrible condition—practically falling down from decades of neglect. But the views were spectacular; I loved the light. And within five minutes I knew I'd made the right decision.

Everything had to go. Walls, floors, doors, bathrooms—I didn't keep a thing. When we put it back together, I combined part of the living room with a bedroom to shape a big master suite and created capacious guest quarters—three bedrooms became two, but the new spaces are more comfortable and luxurious. I also restyled the interior, retaining the flavor of the original but making the details simpler and the look more contemporary.

Decoratively, the rooms reflect my passion for ancient cultures and intriguing objects—rare and individual. I didn't want to make a home where people were afraid to put their feet up. The result, I believe, is a place that is serene, welcoming, and populated by objects, artworks, and furnishings that speak of many times and cultures.

When I work for clients, I am totally in their zone. But when working for oneself, anything goes. A lot of designers say that it's difficult to create their own places, but I thoroughly enjoyed the experience—and, most important, I genuinely love to come home.

OPPOSITE: *The English bookcase in the foyer contains my collection of Islamic pottery, crafted between the eighth and twelfth centuries. A pair of nineteenth-century Chinese calligraphy panels, created for the Middle Eastern market, frame the giltwood Rococo mirror.* OVERLEAF: *Though the two Italian chaise longues are contemporary, they evince a 1930s flavor, which suits the style of my living room.*

ABOVE: *Two Regency armchairs upholstered in heather-colored leather stand before an eighteenth-century French limestone fireplace. A Robert Motherwell lithograph hangs beside an oil depicting a Mediterranean harbor scene.* OPPOSITE: *A work by Elger Esser anchors the sofa wall.*

Treasures gathered
over decades of travel—
interesting and
unique—are excellent
companions.

RIGHT: *An Italian eighteenth-century trestle table and an English
drop-leaf with Chinese Chippendale details flank the living room
sofa. My beloved Ellsworth Kelly hangs above the Italian cabinet; the
circles in the hallway were painted by Frank Stella.*

ABOVE AND OPPOSITE: *For my intimate dining room, I designed decorative plasterwork panels for the walls to establish a nineteenth-century aesthetic within a contemporary setting. The table—a George III Irish three-pillar executed in mahogany circa 1790—is paired with replicas of 1920s French chairs. The chandelier I found in Paris; the magnificent overmantel looms above a nineteenth-century English sideboard.*

I combine many global elements into my design palette; somehow the overall effect is distinctly American. Perhaps only a democracy can accept so much diversity so easily.

RIGHT: *A painting by Wolf Kahn, set against a backdrop of Tunisian tiles, is a pleasure to look at while I'm cooking. A vintage chandelier from the French firm Bagues hangs above the custom-designed marble-and-walnut island.*

RIGHT: *I added walnut paneling to the library—it really warms up the room—and then contrasted it with the antique Belgian tiles of the fireplace surround. The painting above it, by George Inness Sr., dates from 1880, and the hanging textile is actually an antique saddle from northwest Persia.*

ABOVE: *The study adjoins the master bedroom, which is nice when I'm working late at night.* OPPOSITE: *In the hallway leading to the bedroom, I placed a giltwood Rococo table and a joyful plein-air landscape by the artist Alexander Loemans.*

RIGHT: *The creams and soft pinks in the master bedroom are reminiscent of the morning light. Just so things don't become too soothing, I set a pair of colorful Cy Twomblys atop a nineteenth-century bureau de dame and an eighteenth-century Italian chest of drawers.* OVERLEAF: *Just inside the door to the bedroom is a Dutch Baroque carved giltwood mirror paired with a chrome-and-cut-glass lamp. Across the room, above a fauteuil, hangs a circa 1837 chalk study of a tree branch.*

ABOVE: *The bathroom is hard-edged—functional and modern—yet tactile, softened with materials and art.*
OPPOSITE: *The guest bedroom is small, but built-ins create extra sleeping areas. I designed the Spanish-Moorish headboard to fit the smaller space and encourage an exotic experience.*

CASUAL COMFORTS

I love refinement and elegance, but I love being casual even more. To me, casual equals comfort—a casual place invites you in and makes you really feel at ease. I was once interviewed by potential clients whose Park Avenue apartment had been impeccably done—everything was perfectly arranged, every object had a pedigree. The problem was that the design felt suffocating even to the residents, who had trouble finding a cozy place to sit. An interior can be well thought out and carefully detailed but still relaxed and unpretentious in a way that makes it feel like a true and welcoming home.

Just as my formal interiors come from formal architecture, my casual designs sit comfortably within a more relaxed shell. Often I will work with an architect to achieve this, as when I transformed a dark-paneled sixties-era beach house into a light, bright residence that recalled an early-twentieth-century seaside bungalow. Casual design can also be sweet (as opposed to cute): blue-jean colors, objects and antiques that aren't so precious.

There is also the "formally informal" interior, in which the more serious elements of a home are rendered in a casual way—wicker furnishings as opposed to upholstered pieces, sisal rugs, wrought-iron rather than crystal chandeliers. Another strategy I use is to mix in a traditional object, like a Biedermeier chaise, that was considered informal in its day, to create a dialogue across time.

Whatever the direction, the most important thing is to avoid fashioning a showplace. In a casual interior, everything is meant to look good, to feel good—and to be well and lovingly used.

OPPOSITE: *Simple white-painted chairs, a French provincial bench and farm table, a Turkish wall hanging serving as a table linen: nothing in this dining area is fancy or pretentious, and it is all a pleasure to enjoy.*

Casual architecture breeds casual interiors. Classic American post-and-beam construction, for instance, painted a fresh, bright white, suggests solidity, simplicity, and the presence of the craftsman's hand.

RIGHT: *The living room of this Delaware beach house originally featured dark paneling. First we transformed it into a bright and inviting seaside cottage. Then I warmed up the space with soft colors and welcoming textures. An unframed oil painting adds a note of informality.*

ABOVE AND OPPOSITE: *An essential component of casualness is ease of use. In this living room beside the sea, the fabrics are sturdy and easy to care for, from the overstuffed throw pillows to the linen-and-cotton rug.*

ABOVE AND OPPOSITE: *We eliminated the upper part of the kitchen walls in the Delaware beach house, at once increasing the easygoing air and opening the room to abundant natural light and views. The bluestone countertops and backsplash remind me of the sea-smoothed stones on the beach.*

ABOVE: *I rendered the Delaware bathroom in refreshing layers of white.* OPPOSITE: *The bedroom is characterized by lush layers of comfortable Italian linens, an Aubusson carpet, and—at the foot of the bed—a nineteenth-century French chaise.*

ABOVE: *Casual can still be beautiful, as suggested by the antique Turkish suzani at the foot of the bed in the cottage in Delaware.*
OPPOSITE: *An informal environment encourages the use of beloved objects—like decorative plates and a pitcher-and-washbowl set—that otherwise might remain in the closet.*

Formal houses may contain informal spaces. The challenge lies in creating an effective aesthetic bridge between the two, with vintage furniture pieces, architectural references, or perhaps artworks. If the mix is right, the mood remains relaxed.

RIGHT: *The decor in a sunroom in Chevy Chase—notably the antique wicker furniture, which I found, and left, white-painted, and the Biedermeier chaise—amplifies the early-twentieth-century, Arts and Crafts flavor of the architecture.*

When a room opens onto a garden, a delightful casualness is virtually a given— as is designing an indoor/outdoor space. But none of this means that the room can't contain serious elements as well.

LEFT: *For this living room in a newly built Long Island house, my clients requested "relaxed formality." I began with the superlative nineteenth-century Bakshaish rug, across which a pair of loosely upholstered sofas face one another.*

ABOVE: *I relaxed the classical flavor of the architecture in this Chevy Chase breakfast room with a pair of rustic French corner cabinets.* OPPOSITE: *What was once the dark porch of a farmhouse on the eastern shore of Maryland was converted into a formally arranged room that, thanks to its contents, feels informal: wicker furnishings, a sisal rug, a simple lantern chandelier.*

Every culture has its own definition of casual style—and designing for people from different cultures requires understanding that definition and adapting it to a family's preferences and needs.

LEFT: *This McLean, Virginia, family room features a nineteenth-century kilim carpet; the French sleigh bed is adorned with sumptuous pillows; and a pair of wicker chairs and a sofa are separated by an adjustable-height coffee table.*

ABOVE AND OPPOSITE: *In the family room of a Sands Point, New York, residence, an English nineteenth-century hallway bench paired with a walnut table establishes a multipurpose zone—breakfast, games, homework—for the family's children. The 1950s chandelier I found in Paris.*

ABOVE: *In this tiny living room in a Rehoboth, Delaware, beach house, I deliberately placed a lot of furniture—in part because, with three children, my clients needed it, but also to make the space feel inviting and comfortable.* OPPOSITE: *The light yellow toile in this cozy guest bedroom, in a house on the eastern shore of Maryland, covers not just the walls but the ceiling. The natural light creates a soothing mood.*

ARTFUL TEXTILES

Despite being in a somewhat social profession, I am a shy person. When I walk into a room, I keep my eyes lowered—and so the first thing I see is the rug. I have learned something: not everyone is outgoing, but everyone wants to feel welcome—and if you have a beautiful rug, even a shy person with downcast eyes will be very much at home.

I adore rugs. They are the life, the soul, of any residence. And they are always the way I start—the best method I know to give character and color to a space. Contrary to what many people believe, rugs are also easy to work with decoratively. Whatever the objects or furnishings you put on top of them, whatever the style or color scheme, they always work—because rugs remain as beautiful, and appropriate, as great paintings.

I use textiles on walls as well, such as European tapestries and Turkish suzanis, but I have to think carefully because it is a commitment that defines a room. Yet a wall-size tapestry can make a small space seem much bigger, and soft antique wall hangings work beautifully with modern clean-lined furnishings. Like the often exotic, strongly graphic chandeliers and fixtures that work in counterpoint to my floor coverings, such objects introduce personality and narrative into a space—even one that's otherwise empty.

I have never been partial to florals or manufactured patterns. Unique textiles are my chintzes—fabrics that are not about attaching oneself to a well-known brand or style cue but remain as individual as the people whose spaces they enliven.

OPPOSITE: *For a child's room in a house in Chevy Chase, Maryland, I adorned an antique French sleigh bed with a richly embroidered Turkish suzani. The textile was originally a wall hanging—and thus too small for the bed—so I added the lower panel to create an ample coverlet.*

ABOVE AND OPPOSITE: *This glass-enclosed sunroom in a historic house designed by John Russell Pope combines a number of exotic elements—an antique Malayer carpet, nineteenth-century Anglo-Indian plantation chairs, a pierced-metal-and-glass Moroccan chandelier—for my world-traveling clients. The Louis XVI–style giltwood sofa is paired with a table made from a beautifully weathered slab of oak I found in Jaipur.*

ABOVE AND OPPOSITE: *I layered a small family room office in a beach house in Delaware with an array of fabrics, colors, and fixtures. An antique suzani commands one wall; before the overstuffed sofa, upholstered in toile, the custom ottoman is covered with a Persian sofra, a hand-embroidered textile. The nineteenth-century genre painting, depicting a waterfront in the American northeast, captures the spirit of this simple cottage.*

My projects are most successful
when contemporary style is
combined with classical elements
and antiques reflecting the
influences of many cultures.
This mix of places and periods,
understated yet vivid,
produces a quality I describe
as "modern simplicity."

RIGHT: *To complement the proportions of this long and narrow
sitting room, I set nineteenth-century Japanese painted wood cabinets
on either side of the fireplace. The simple sofa, from Holly Hunt,
and the upholstered ottoman I designed, which provides additional
seating, integrate easily into the Asian-influenced interior.*

ABOVE AND OPPOSITE: *A superb nineteenth-century copper lantern from Syria adorns this McLean, Virginia, dining room. The embroidered and painted Chinese wall hanging complements the rich wood pieces and soft wall color. For more informal, intimate meals, I created a second, smaller dining area by a window, pairing a comfortable settee with a late-eighteenth-century English side table with a scalloped top.*

ABOVE AND OPPOSITE: *This small foyer in the house in McLean, Virginia, is a cornucopia of treasures, among them a pair of English armchairs, a nineteenth-century Syrian chest of drawers with mother-of-pearl inlay, and a nineteenth-century Persian portrait of a Kajar emperor. The colorful image of an embracing couple, suspended between the stair and an antique American bench, is painted on a board-mounted Persian tile.*

ABOVE AND OPPOSITE: *I discovered the Art Nouveau decorative tiles flanking the fire box in the McLean, Virginia, house in a private collection and paired them with contemporary tiles in a complementary color. I installed shelving in a dining room niche to display my clients' extensive assembly of Persian and Syrian artifacts.*

ABOVE AND OPPOSITE: *This richly textured dining room, in a New York apartment, features a wall hanging made from an eighteenth-century silk robe, an early-twentieth-century Turkish textile on the table, a corner cabinet from Sweden, and multiple objects from my clients' collections.*

Layering fabrics and
patterns—simple modern
shades, lightly pooled
draperies, upholstered chairs,
embroidered pillows—can
make the most formal room
feel relaxed and inviting.

RIGHT: *There's a delicacy to this Long Island living room,*
with its nineteenth-century embroidered armchairs,
French chinoiserie table with cabriole legs, and custom velvet
ottoman, that relaxes and sweetens its formality.

174   INTERIOR VISIONS

I like to put large
furniture—and
sometimes a lot of
it—in small spaces.
Under the right
circumstances, bigger
and busier can
indeed be better.

RIGHT: *The white-painted four-poster in a
bedroom in Rehoboth, Delaware, a reproduction
of an American bed from the Colonial era, pairs
well with the weathered French provincial table
beside it. The simplicity of the surrounding objects
highlights the lamp's modern elegance.*

ABOVE AND OPPOSITE: *A close look at a nineteenth-century Syrian mirror reveals the stunning intricacy of its mother-of-pearl and wood inlay. A distant view of a similarly crafted piece—like this chest of drawers—shows the larger pattern more readily than the particulars.*

Variety and interest can be drawn from the most subtle of differences. Multiple shades of cream—each, perhaps, in a differently textured natural fabric—create a captivating palette.

RIGHT: *In the master suite of a Rehoboth, Delaware, residence, lightly enclosing panels on the headboard make the bed feel cozier—a room within a room. Industrial-style nickel-finished swing-arm lamps contrast with a delicately embroidered eighteenth-century Turkish throw hanging behind the bed.*

ABOVE AND OPPOSITE: *The typical male doesn't linger over his toilette. But this European-style man's bath—its Roman influences enlivened with Middle Eastern fabrics and furnishings—makes a strong argument for spending more time in the tub.*

RIGHT: *In this guest room, in New York's Museum Tower, an antique English gilt mirror suspended above the two-poster bed captures the daylight. Late-eighteenth-century Chinese wood tables serve as nightstands, and a birdcage—gathered in the course of my client's travels—perches before the window.*

ABOVE AND OPPOSITE: *While both of the nightstands in the Museum Tower guest room are Chinese, they are from slightly different periods and depart subtly from one another in design.* OVERLEAF: *Both the headboard and the X-shaped ottoman in this Chevy Chase master bedroom were designed for the space, as was the bolster made from nineteenth-century Italian linen.*

To me, a ceiling that hasn't received an appropriate decorative treatment feels unfinished and makes a room less welcoming. Ceilings, floors, and walls work well when treated as one.

RIGHT: *I upholstered this entire guest room in Chevy Chase, Maryland, in blue-and-white toile to create an exceptionally cozy and soothing cocoon. A nineteenth-century French bergère offers an alternative to the bed.*
OVERLEAF: *In a former industrial building in Baltimore, I contrasted the exposed ductwork in a guest bedroom with a Portuguese bed, an eighteenth-century giltwood floral-patterned mirror, and an early-twentieth-century French chandelier.*

ABOVE AND OPPOSITE: *Three drapery panels suspended from rods attached to the ceiling semienclose the bed and make a small master bedroom in Baltimore feel larger. An Empire cast-metal candelabra forms a halo above the pillows.*

COUNTRY SCENES

When it comes to design, I have no rules—and this is especially true when I work on country houses, which often repeat the style clichés associated with their location. My solution is to see a residence not as belonging to a specific place but rather as the type of "country house" that could be found anywhere in the world.

A good example is the home I designed, on a 180-acre horse farm in Kentucky, for a companionable family with a love of entertaining. When we first spoke about the project, they envisioned having several dining areas and inviting friends over for feasts after polo matches, then relaxing comfortably and informally in overstuffed chairs. What they didn't want was a typical "horse farm in bluegrass country" design. By applying a global vision, I was able to combine, in unexpected ways, elements from multiple cultures.

Consider the pendant light fixture above one of the dining tables. It's a Turkish oil lamp from the 1800s—one that, in a country house in another time and place, served precisely the same function. It's unusual, yet it works because it has a secret appropriateness to its setting.

Such an approach allowed me to introduce kilim rugs and suzani tapestries, an antique Chinese jar and a nineteenth-century Italian mirror. And by opening the door to a flexible way of looking at things, I felt free to bring in objects that, truthfully, one would never find in a farmhouse, like the Venetian chandelier in the master suite—a burst of glamour in a rustic setting.

If something looks and feels right, then why not use it? It's a design principle that is usefully applied in the country, but it finds its way into all of my work.

OPPOSITE: *Though this horse farm, in a particularly sylvan section of Kentucky's bluegrass country, is very much rooted in a sense of place, I collaborated with my clients to create a series of strongly international interiors.*

ABOVE: *For the farmhouse's covered porch, I chose to maintain a simple rustic feel. Chairs inlaid with mother-of-pearl from Syria flank an African farm table topped with Chinese boxes. The ornate candlesticks come from Italy.*
OPPOSITE: *During polo season, when big parties are the norm, the long banquet table easily seats eighteen people; four circular tables surrounding it provide more intimate alternatives.*

My world-traveling clients embraced the idea of a design that gathered elements from multiple cultures, some from their journeys, others—like the cocktail tables inlaid with nineteenth-century Indian sandstone screens—brought by me to the global table.

RIGHT: *The farm's north terrace features wrought-iron furniture and cushions upholstered in an outdoors-friendly linen blend. Though the nineteenth-century Persian copper tray above the fireplace is permanent, my clients roll up the carpet when the weather takes a turn for the worse.*

ABOVE: *The porch overlooks a pond, beyond which fenced pastures unfold.* OPPOSITE: *A Chinese daybed with pillows from a cornucopia of countries adorns the farmhouse's main entrance.*

"Country" is as much a state of mind as a specific style—and the content of a country house can express that spirit in multiple ways. Refined multicultural objects, for instance, may complement a rustic flavor.

RIGHT: *This intimate indoor dining room features a nineteenth-century Turkish oil lamp as a chandelier—entirely appropriate to a contemporary farmhouse, since it served the same function in the past. The carpet is an antique Serapi.*
OVERLEAF: *A quiet corner in the dining room features antique Chinese ceramic chargers on the wall. A nineteenth-century French mirror in the sitting room—stripped of paint and beautifully patinated—hangs above a table from the same place and period.*

When things aren't so serious, it can be easier to make use of every part of a dwelling. In a country house, it's especially pleasurable to be able to settle down anywhere and relax.

RIGHT: *In a transitional space between the farmhouse's public rooms and master suite, I created a cozy sitting room focused on a Persian kilim and comfortable pillows.*

PEOPLE WE KNOW, HORSES THEY LOVE

ABOVE: *Family photos and drawings form a welcoming presence in the entry to the master suite.* OPPOSITE: *I found the lamp on the sofa table in the sitting area in a local shop.* OVERLEAF: *Beneath the rough-hewn beams of the master suite are such precious objects as delicate porcelains on the cocktail table and a superlative oil by Milton Avery above the fireplace.*

In a country house a
room can assert its
qualities in many ways—
and with clients who are
collectors, the tone will
be richly personal.

RIGHT: *For the master suite, with its soaring windows*
and fourteen-foot ceilings, I couldn't resist a manorial
treatment. A seventeenth-century Flemish tapestry
featuring a hunting scene serves as a headboard, and a
brilliant Murano crystal chandelier is suspended above.
Brown linen drapes enhance the chamber's authority.

ABOVE AND OPPOSITE: *On and around a magnificent carved walnut desk in the master suite is my clients' collection of Asian ceramics. The lamp was fashioned from a Chinese wallpaper roll.*

RIGHT: *Brilliant blue doors enliven the farmhouse's mudroom. In case people need a reminder to remove their boots, there's a handwoven Persian rug.*
OVERLEAF: *On the simple painted American desk in the wife's dressing room, a handcrafted vase and a vividly glazed lamp from the 1940s add a touch of glamour (enhanced by the flowing draperies).*

ACKNOWLEDGMENTS

Interior Visions owes its life to many creative, resourceful, and supportive individuals, and it is a pleasure to thank them here. My dear colleague, graphic designer David Ashton, encouraged me to undertake this book. It was his idea, and I'm especially grateful for it.

The photographers Erik Kvalisk and Scott Frances captured my work beautifully. Their understanding of light, color, and narrative not only makes every room look good but shows how it feels to inhabit it—thank you both.

My thanks as well to Doug Turshen, whose book design is rich and expressive, and Marc Kristal, an eloquent and reflective writer who made sense of all my thoughts. Bert Winchester of Winchester Construction built and renovated a lot of my work with superior quality and integrity.

A special thank you to my agent, Jill Cohen, a thoughtful, sincere, and wonderful person, who carried me through the complex and unfamiliar process of creating a book with good humor and unflagging energy and made the experience meaningful and worthwhile. Anyone would be lucky to work with Jill. I am forever indebted to her.

My deep gratitude to all the people in my office. Without their help and support, none of my projects would have come to fruition.

I must express my thanks to Gianfranco Monacelli and the superb editors at The Monacelli Press for their support and encouragement.

To a most inspiring figure: Paige Rense of *Architectural Digest.* Her vision has single-handedly shaped contemporary design and architecture. I am deeply grateful to her for taking an interest in my work and believing that I had a future at a time when I was a relatively unknown practitioner.

My thanks to an extremely talented architect, Wayne Good, whose work always inspires me, for all the wonderful projects on which we continue to work. My deepest gratitude to the brilliant Allan Greenberg, whom I love and respect for his expertise at his craft—I believe he is the very best of architects—and also for his kindness, sincerity, and genuineness, which shine through his work and inspire me. I owe him so much.

Finally, I would like to express my gratitude to the many beautiful cultures and lands that have inspired my work; to my clients who entrusted me with their most personal and intimate spaces and challenged me to make each and every home unique and personal; to my three wonderful children, Ahmad, Bana, and Walid, for the joy they bring to my life; and to God, who lifts me up, gives me strength, and provides the truest inspiration.

Copyright © 2011 by Mona Hajj and The Monacelli
Press, a division of Random House, Inc.

All rights reserved. Published in the United States
by The Monacelli Press, a division of Random
House, Inc., New York

The Monacelli Press and the M design are
registered trademarks of Random House, Inc.

Library of Congress Cataloging-in-Publication Data
Hajj, Mona.
Interior visions / Mona Hajj ; foreword by Allan
Greenberg ; text written with Marc Kristal.—1st ed.
p.   cm.
ISBN 978-1-58093-320-9
1. Hajj, Mona—Themes, motives. 2. Interior
decoration—Themes, motives. I. Kristal, Marc.
II. Title.
NK2004.3.H355A4   2011
747.092—dc22   2010043960

Printed in China

www.monacellipress.com

10 9 8 7 6 5 4 3 2 1
First edition

Designed by Doug Turshen with David Huang

Photography Credits
Numbers refer to page numbers.

Big Blue Photography: 62, 63

Pieter Estersohn: 2, 13, 15, 16, 17, 53, 55, 69, 70, 71,
77, 79, 81, 82, 160, 161, 165, 179

Scott Frances: 4, 11, 22–23, 24, 25, 26–27, 29, 30,
31, 32–33, 35, 37, 113, 114–15, 116, 117, 119, 120, 121,
123, 125, 126, 127, 129, 130, 131, 132, 133, 147, 159,
188–89, 191

Erik Kvalsvik: 9, 18, 19, 20, 21, 38, 39, 41, 42, 43,
44, 45, 46, 47, 50, 51, 56–57, 58, 59, 60, 61, 64, 65,
66, 67, 72, 74, 75, 83, 84, 85, 87, 91, 92, 93, 94, 97,
98, 99, 100, 101, 103, 104, 105, 106, 107, 108, 109,
111, 135, 137, 138, 139, 140, 141, 142, 143, 144, 145,
148–49, 150, 151, 152, 154, 155, 156, 157, 162, 163,
166, 167, 168, 169, 170, 171, 172, 173, 175, 177, 178,
181, 182, 183, 185, 186, 187, 192, 193, 194, 195, 197,
198, 199, 201, 202, 203, 205, 206, 207, 209, 210,
211, 212, 213, 215, 216, 217, 219, 220, 221, 223

Author photograph by Richard Anderson